Brood

MONGREL EMPIRE PRESS
NORMAN, OKLAHOMA, UNITED STATES OF AMERICA

2015

FIRST EDITION, 2015

Brood
© 2015 by C. R. Resetarits

ISBN 9978-0-9903204-4-9

Cover Art
Zeus opening a bisected egg labelled *Ex ovo omnia*:
'Everything from the egg'
frontispiece from William Harvey, *De generatione animalium* (1651)

MONGREL EMPIRE PRESS
NORMAN, OK

ONLINE CATALOGUE: WWW.MONGRELEMPIRE.ORG

This publisher is a proud member of

[clmp]

COUNCIL OF LITERARY MAGAZINES & PRESSES
w w w . c l m p . o r g

Book Design: Mongrel Empire Press using iWork Pages

BROOD
noun
1. a number of ideas, metaphors, or eggs produced or hatched at one time.
2. a breed, species, group, or kind: The poem exhibited a brood of piquant words.

verb (with object)
3. to sit upon; incubate.
4. to warm, protect, or cover with the wings, body, or objective correlative.
5. to think or worry persistently or moodily about; to ponder; to poem.

verb (without object)
6. to sit upon; incubate.
7. to dwell on a subject or to meditate with morbid and/or poetic persistence.

adjective
8. kept for breeding: She kept her brood poems cooped up in a warm and cozy lower drawer.

Grateful acknowledgment is made to the following journals.

"Actor's Studio," *Ballard Street Poetry Journal* (Sept. 2012); "Alice at Lessons," *Perfume River Poetry Review* (2013); "Arroyo," *Talking Sticks: Native Arts Quarterly* 13.3 (2010); "Auspicium," *Lalitamba Magazine* (2014); "Breakfast midway to Bierstadt Lake," *Ruminate* (Summer 2011); "Bull," *Hawai'i Review* 81 (2014);"Compass," *Helix* (Fall 2012); "Cubist Lovers," *Vagabonds: Anthology of the Mad Ones* 3, no. 1 (Weasel Press, 2014); "Derby," [formerly "The Roller Derby"], *Pacific Review* (Spring 2015); "Dog Gone," *Dogs Singing Anthology* (Cliffs of Moher, Ireland: Salmon Poetry Ltd., 2010); "Echo," *Cloudbank* (November 2012); "Elegy," *Talking Sticks: Native Arts Quarterly* 13.3 (2010); "Everett Ruess," *Weber—The Contemporary West* (2013); "Falling," *Kindred Magazine* (October 2013); "Fits and Starts," *Midnight Circus: Rejected Dreams* (2014); "Flint Hills," *Florida Review* Native Writing Issue (Summer 2010); "Hovenweep," *Kestrel* (Fall 2013); "Lake," *Seeding the Snow* (2012) and a variant version "Qui Ho Lake" in *Ancient Heart Magazine* (Spring 2007); "Looking West," *Weber—The Contemporary West* (2013); "Mick," *Clockhouse Review* (2013); "Sea Change," *Cradle Songs: The Motherhood Anthology* (Quill and Parchment 2012); "Songs," *Anak Sastra* 16 (2014); "Summer Turbulence" [formerly "Turbulence"], *Lines Underwater*, ed. Laura Seymour and Kirsten Tambling (London: Tyburn Tree, 2013); "Territories," *Florida Review* Native Writing Issue (Summer 2010); "Watercress," *Owen Wister Review* (2014).

Contents

Brood

C. R. Resetarits

Actor's Studio

Urban street. Busy clan of erudites
vivisecting last night's upstart play:
sister mothers, big bros, waify niece.
    "Ah bloomy-blooms," says waif, blossom-snatching
the jacaranda of Beverly Grove.
This clan prefers the Blooms of Joyce
and holds to fire any actor's brogue.
    "Bloomy-drops like candy hearts,
like dum-dum pops, like pollylops,
from blooming hills and Bloomingdales,"
our girly quips and skips.
    "Millefleur," a mother notes—
"one thousand puffs on leaf green stems
like actor's flourish of accents at last night's . . .
    "Oh Milly, Molly, fleurs and follys!
Bloomy-dums from BLOOMINGDALES.
Get it? Get it? Don't you see?
Bloomingdales and blooming trees!"
the niece explains with mild reproof
for opaque mams and brother nits.
    They stop mid-parsing to watch her spin.
Most amused by her supple mind,
the way her words play hide and seek,
play thinking of, come ready or not,
    like magic from her Play-doh mind.
She grins and revels on center stage.
City child spins city script. Building plots
on flowering twigs, on metaflorals,
      on words that bloom, invoking her voice,
        her audience.

Alice at Lessons

We sit by the river, pupil and tutor.

"There are many fine trees here. Now . . ."

I have to interrupt, to expressed my surprise at the placement of trees between the runs of listing walls, which are all the same yellow-red burnt brick, stolen from some demolished place, from some equally demolished time, the placement I insist is too intentional for such a haphazard city.

"Midhat Pasha," my tutor instructs, "a great reforming governor of the previous century, planned to tear down the remaining fortress walls of the ancient city and replace them with parkways and esplanades, along the lines of many European cities, and while his plans were never completed, their remnants, like the remnants of all great reformers before him for dozens of millennia flourish with or without him, amidst the rubble of ages, rising green and fragrant and renewed, gardens and groves, oleander, orange, pomegranate, fig, lemon, date-palm."

"How familiar," I offer as if my thoughts are swallow flights, "the mix of odors, the slow burn of ancients, the sweet tease of blooms, the always old and the always new."

"No, no, no," my tutor blows, "always neither, never either. Listen, girl, and name those trees."

I circle and drop the names upon his head like silt and clay falling from my glimmer wings as I glide ever higher in the warm wind of his bellows.

Arroyo

Not clean but splattered
from rain that hits these Western roads
from head to toe the season's
wind and rain mock this place, this time,
    this dirty game.
Ash to ash, like alchemist twins
blackened hearth and cleansing lies
the gravity of me and man
the thing that follows foot to ground
to let go all that goes to ground
when days are done
    but, sometimes, I go now
in search of proofs arroyos lend.

So no, not clean but most obscenely drenched
in sweat and dirt and dew
from morning slides down wrinkling land
    listen
vesper, lark, or sparrow hawk—
their fine thin songs stitch pinyon trees
to pellucid skies. Marvel, trace,
hair full of twigs from rushing
headfirst chokecherry shrubs.
Not clean, but bramble burred,
next not to heaven and what's more
    glad, not next,
but dead on in the gulch
dirt smearing forehead, lips, and breast.

Auspicium

Birds who sky skim as if
corps de ballet,
Cirque de Soleil.
First blush is envy
but on review I'm
numbed by numbers
gagged by gaggles
until
one bird spotted
flying wind
the wrong way.
Awkward, unlovely,
a salve all the same
for sore eyes wearied
at the bluing threat
of dawn's dormers
and blank parchment.

Breakfast Midway to Bierstadt Lake

What pretty little leaves
the aspen have—like
limes or lemons or
at a distance
for a moment
clementines.

They pour down mountains
down burnt toast crevasses
the zigzag of ill-cut loafs
like molten marmalades
shimmering for waking eyes
dancing for hungry tongues.

Broken Stick

Trace compass spinning
trace gathering clouds
trace garbage gathering
trace edge unraveling
trace ancient mounds:
Monk, Angel, Bottle Creek.

Trace running water run to ground,
to bones, to rock, to old corn crops
to withdraw from this to other worlds.

But we are left below, behind
to pray not bested by brutal skies
by falcon dancers throwing stones
our words and rites
our broken spears
our severed heads
are shadow tales
are ancient markers
to ill-lit passes and
forgotten trails.

Brood

Tossing art from
boy to boy
my twinning sons
of different druthers—
gadfly Peter and
somber Paul.

Wax and wane
feed growing brood:
disciplined Paul
takes earth and sea
and born of air
his brother Pan.

Looking back,
fault-etched scapes of
Matisse yellow and
Van Gogh blue—
back roads wavy
as old regrets.

The bubbling arts
of hat and sleeve:
deft slights of hand
and shifting feet
one thumb in pie
one toe in peat.

Bull

This time last year the Bull's third electroshock was misapplied. What had til then been remedy—brute wind to low-land fog—dropped a cloud, a thick woolly net to mood and mind. Court still gathered at Cedar Street

but the Bull moved mired: nooscopic hoofs through salt marsh muck. Slowly but slowly, he found his way, a thread of longing left by ocean breeze.

Number four was better tracked and brought again that good clean gray to our pie-eyed christ, our suffering beast of brackishness.

Compass

Each new journey begins an ancient compass:
there are knobby, snowstorm, pinescape sways and
hardwood branches shaking clear shiny icewares
whenever winds tumble down ancient river basins;

there are wisteria binding and muffling southern clines
and palmetto, yellow pine, and live oak shrugging, slowly,
when springtime games begin again, so soon;

there are blue-ridge shadows mocking low clouds, lost worlds,
while old ocean floors roll out between, beyond, offering
gods all their own and gardens of sandstone, salt, and shale.

Note how in red gardens the off-greens of cacti and sage play
like puns or spirit lore. Like me, they are awkward, resilient but
fanciful too, for when warm winds launch cottonwood seeds,
we, for a moment, see a riddle of snow in empty, desert skies.

Cubist Lovers

The setting is Clovis Sagot's gallery—a clown's apothecary recast as artistic alchemy. There the faux Egyptian figures under the Picassos are a wry reflection of Rousseau's sales pitch: "Greats of our time—you Egyptian, the Modern mine."

Our hero is just back from the Valley of Kings to hawk his amulets and ancient fake things when a lovely girl stumbles in at the jester's door. She moves like a crane, dark plume, oddly balanced yet plumb. He notes absinthe fumes and a licorice tongue skimming shamrock lips. She weaves, sighs and sings, "How brilliant your charms lined up in a row."

He turns his best smile, best barker's pitch, and dips mesmeric quill in her unctuous ink.

"So delicate and rare. In moonlight they dance; in sunlight spin. Have you a window from which to display? A candle-lit niche—with your beautiful face—a halo of wonder, almost. Come, touch, know, guess their secrets, their weight.

She takes an amulet into her hand, face flushing, slant eyes glazed with effort, and then she drops it into the pocket of her coat, flashes an empty palm, smiles, walks away.

Our boy is pleased. Often after he spots her in town. She is shy, sly. She touches her pocket with fingers as small and delicate as beguiling white lies. He follows, he paints, he captures her essence but never her heart: gold eyes, emerald mouth, and a lovely black-scarlet slash of secrets.

Cut Outs

Sissy bacon in slick hot nap
moist and limp and wrinkling.
While she sleeps, I'm up to steal
you where you're full inclined to go.

A shoebox from another time
snapshots, ribbons, paper dolls
but paper play is timeless, true,
and with my wiles I lure you in—
we disappear, we are complete
paper playing across your bed.

What a shame the piglet never knew
those paper faces, paper clothes,
their muted shades of elegance
their tale of longing, love, and loss.
The soldier's stance with hat cocked so.
The lady's gown and fine fox wrap.
He leaves at dawn, and so they dance.

I would lend pork our paper ways
but friends and dying cleared your things
thorough cruel, they went too far,
and banned poor pig from paper shores
as if a purge could clear intrigue,
as if a blitz could heal a war,
trapping me with me alone
to disappear through paper doors.

Derby

Ringside a woman in dotted dress
is euphoria-faced, beset by fleshy-cheeked
men bespectacled, beflashing their glee
like fish scales across this moony star night.

This night, flash bulbs and cat calls and muses
on steel round a slope wood ring round
the Rosies and Vals, the Midges and Gers
round, round, round regular girls.

This night, silk bloomers and knee pads,
speed jams, elbows and waist whips,
apple bottoms flung over apple-cart
railings, over high-flying wheel kicks.

The poses poetic: grecian graceful,
roman square. Toughie's back bent like
Discobolos anchoring Poussin arms.
And the while steel sounds rolling through

nonsensical decks. The sirens are river-town wits
winged for rounding my childhood's laugh track.

Dog Gone

My dog has gone after dreams again.
He stops a moment to contemplate
a scrubbing at the garden hedge
then through he darts—one of his many
alchemist skills. My dog is gone next
piney gust, next whorl of leaves.

We both ramble worlds too easily
called out as we are by shifting breeze.
His cosmos rife with shooting smells,
with riffs of *musica universalis*
or the lopping beat of spaniel ears.
A kin to my own palimpsestic ways,
our cold dark kennings, our ionized hearts,
from dodging bits of broken stars.

But this braid heathland holds acres of chance,
our cloudless sky pales blue so blue that shamed
rust hills take violet veil, and light too bright
for eyes and mind—lemon pith white—
leaves thought clean and spare as nova grace.

And there is my dog gone far afield,
a black feather blown over a gold-green land.
He's worn and ready for fate to move.
Only once past wasted does he think of me,
only once the wind has gathered and turned—
drowning smells and harms and words.
I'll meet him halfway, whistle him home.
We'll both sleep deep still battling stars.

Echo

I rediscovered ears today.
Found them on my dusty floor.
They might have dropped
years ago so curiously
odd they seemed.
But I do faintly recall
how the other senses
came to life when hearing
was around, and round it was
for all the broken pieces
were curved like tiny bowls
for holding hints and whispers.

There were dusty pieces
under my reading chair,
under the tire swing,
among my dusty books.
I remember when these too
were sounding shells
where wonder notes
were caught and brewed.
But what is this quiet, then,
but a different soup.
You cannot quiet past
traffic, birds, or faltering steps
past words once fallen or
hesitation's breath.

And even if these escape some flint
walled garden, some broad moor walk,
there would still be
the scratching sounds
of inklets pushing stitches
across the pale half-tones
of linen shades drawn
against babbling dawn.

Elegy

for Wilma Washam Rogers

Whoever is gone
was Loveland born
onyx eyes
ebony hair
Ava Gardner at twenty-eight.

Whoever is gone
fed her papoose
night bottle
in red velvet
and oceans of tuille.

Whoever is gone
was eaten by wolves
inside out
filched by white
shit-face shamans.

Whoever is gone
left reservation child:
alphabet writing,
real ones reflecting,
shoe boxes of art.

Whoever is gone
is recaptured here
in green corn poem
by whoever once feared
leaving and losing most.

Everett Ruess

Promise boy, vagabond
in search of beauty, in beauty's thrall
a sketch pad stuffed in saddlebag,
a block print ink of cypress grove,
a book, a burro, a deck of cards.

Knave, Queen, King, Ace to Ace
for Aces will go either way—
Big Sur or Escalante echoscape:
same saddlebag, same deck of cards,
same boy neglect at marking trail.

Burro, Nemo get left behind
but Everett Ruess is Red Rock bound
down hole, down day, down forking stream
a dropless flow, a moonbeam sea,
Narcissus lost to canyon keeps.

Falling

As soon as the puzzling
first page is solved,
I escape outside
to set the week's laundry
to waft in noon breeze,
to add peeled flesh
to compost stew,
to pour cold coffee
over September's
hybrid teas.

I'm never ready
for the melon-tinged
queries I fail
to catch til then.

It is always the slippage,
the unease suggested
by falling leaves
that sends me back to task.

Fits and Starts

Teacher
who'd rather
not teach
Bartleby, the Scrivener.

Pathetic ghost
at borrowed desk
misfiling
weighty matters.

Poet
jester/seer/fool
awaiting the sails
of day.

Life and death
the color red
a hindrance to
beginning.

Flint Hills

An orange blade cuts west, sends quartz hues to cauterize the
seeping sky. Low amethyst blooms tat the edge of petticoat
whirls. Working this slow mid-grass saloon, each petticoat lifts to
whisper promises and threats of deep-furrowed thighs, high hips,
last-ditch horizons. The sweep of cottonwoods working slipless
beyond the parlor doors skim rivulets of spark in coarse, parched
skins. But the mid-grass hills, their petticoat dews, their rusted
corsets, their busted seams, wear velveteen so easily, brief
gossamer green, a revelry, on thighs and hips, on breasts of flint.

Handkerchief

Sister hers: pretty pictures, bold legends,
grand gestures, tickets, trinkets, children's lore.

I mine: notebooks, datebooks, minor tales,
others' lives, studied scabs, worlds of words.

Dispatched in haste, we started three.
Sister in one hand, me other side.
Long rise of yellow road:
atomic mist, lemon dust,
cornmeal, butter, blackboard chalk.
We three walk, walking, walk away.

Sister hers: gilt, leather, rococo
feather-bed falls
lovely, lovely
lies of land.

I mine: paper, ink, palimpsest
felix culpa
quiet, quiet
sit, stay, speak.

And in between
etiology
long faded past, we started three.
Sister at my side, I at hers
and in between fragrant guile
a handkerchief edged
in sorrow and smiles.

We three still walking, walk, walk away.

Hovenweep

The towers espy two small girls and
a woman gathering ground
cherry, beeweed, wolfberry, sedge
caught up in the folds of black tier skirts
caught up in the folds of high snow hearts.
They feast and dance and weave a dream,
a bent braid to offer gaping kiva.

A dusty land of loss.
One is lost to heaven,
one to ground,
one remains in shagbark bough.

Far away she spies the three:
bent braid whirling
through night's sky bowl
in larkspur blue the three glow stars
in larkspur blue they retake towers.
Braid unfurls and flows, a salve
to those cast back of back beyond
one bough, one sky, one sipapu.

Lake

At night your discarded robe
spreads and swirls on prism air.
Our skins—
sun crinkled, secret shore purled—
call to one another. Come, my love,
your bath is drawn in obsidian
and mist and charcoal edged
in moon and star light.
Please, take your time
delve deep
into our promises. I'll wait.
Provocateur. I'll wait and
judge your care by shadows
for I was instantly yours.

Let's

Please, let's be, we two
in this and that not
in those ways all lofty yours
but once all lowly mine.

Let's run too fast—
let's tumble down—
pine straw paths
live oak lanes.

Please let's
you and me
be wretched
wanton, wrecked,
be lost in longing
and bristling need.

Let's lie in wait
with tickles and slaps
on pins and needles
adrift in the sleek, sly
billows of our
blue lubricity.

Let's be weak,
throw caution,
corsets,
curates to wind.

Feeble-minded,
backward two
who are un- un-
un- un- afraid.

Looking West

Early, so very early, we wait for day,
the coffee shop owner and I. He yak-yaks:
"Told the wife . . . what the hell . . . I hear yah, kid."
At first, as he opens up and I stand aside,
our feedbag-faces are dull, heavy.
It's not lack of sleep. Not only. Doubt maybe.
What if his talky charm, his barker's lure,
escapes him, forsakes him, as I am convinced —
this morning more than most — I've nothing left
worth saying, worth staring through panes,
worth rising so early day on day, year on year.
The owner tries his best stand-up routine:
corporate morons, Middle East fix.
Heard it before and I've concerns of my own.
I'm watching, as always, for the flight
of some sweet, singular bird past
my window seat sky, and I must stay stuck
til I do, as all bust balloons caught by twigs
must stay stuck, left to kite calls and vulture spins
left to high plains taunting skies, this morning
a most curious hue,

        pale blue paling with lemon blush
as the sun threatens noon, stirring
cerulean wisps like my old bedroom curtains
when fluttering, threadbare from lye-wash and line-dries,
smelling of sun, dust and sage, same as
my bedspread and pillow, same as my
dreams when the world could hang
hushed on a white-winged dove's coo
from pecans out my window, when—

there, proof, my mettle,
my darling—
morning's sweet errant bird.

Lowcountry Marsh

Marsh, sounding the Moon at winter,
brings a softened brown-gray that is
different than the ink running
the bright greens of spring
or the red mustard flows
of summer cloud bursts.

Now, wet winter months,
the Ashley and James run through
shadows of fog and cloud. The Sun
leaves to visit older brood so Moon
—a cold blue child—
holds Sun's seat over Heron Island.

Ah, Moon—frightened, frightening—
she is a reluctant beauty but a worthy child.
She waits patiently at the Marsh's edge
clicking her heels against the cord grass
and reeds until they quiver and sing.

Meanwhile

School girls pass
    in pale cotton dresses
slim summer straps
    fine angled bones
long hair caught up
    in mid-June amazement
moon-rising chances
    warm summer eves.

Pearly hued pair
    unsteady gait
becrusted, bespectacled
    bodies bonsai betrayed
their scholarship huddle
    their god damn old bones—
left talking to belts, knees
    feet, sidewalk curbs.

Meanwhile, at banquet
    wedding guests wonder
nibbling at shadows
    sipping white wine.
The bridegroom and bride
    by nature will tarry
caught as they are
    between garden and spire.

Mick

The body of man is like a flicker of lightning
existing only to return to Nothingness.
Like the spring growth that shrivels in autumn.
Waste no thought on the process for it has no purpose,
coming and going like dew.

"The Body of Man," by Van Hanh (d. 1018)
[trans. W. S. Merwin]

A flicker of lightning? Well his smile was all film star flash and young god grin. And this is June sunlight on the St. Louis porch of our great aunt May. Mick stands between his mother and mine with diminutive May and me in front. Mick is khaki clad, cigarette rolling between index and thumb, below vein-wrapped wrists. He has the same black curl mane as his mother and mine, same slant-pierce eyes, hint of mountain mutinies, of unclaimed tribute to walking clans.

As for *existing only to return to Nothingness* what is nothinglike about shrapnel or dragon teeth, what is nothinglike about the earth's most lovely man? Mickey shining pearl in a little girl's lullaby. Mighty Mick all tough muscle and knowing arms that scoop you up to rest on mountain fog, my Cousin Danger, making hearts race and dive for cover.

And *like the spring growth that shrivels in autumn* the things that fall are long hot summers, white Ts, dark tans, aviator shades —wave Mickey wave, turn your flashbulb worthy face my way. Standing next to you is a carnival stroll on the Fourth of July for you are a summer-meant man.

Instead, Mick goes June straight into fall. Instead, Fort Wood and helicopters and passion enough to hang on air. Damsel dancer, dragon flier, knight of flash and flicker.

And then one day out to forward staging, routine maneuvers, one more knight's tale to scoop up soldiers under enemy fire. Copter hovers as six run to jump into the dragon's belly as enemy lacers tat-tat earth to sky. Co-pilot dead right off then a cluster of bullets and dragon scales slice the muscles clean from Mickey's gorgeous scooping arm. With the other he gets airborne to silver stars and morphine drips.

And how does one *waste no thought on the process* the purposeless process? I think we must or lose our summers too, as our Mickeys do. First pain and antidote, then one morphine drip flows quite naturally toward another bourbon bottle, threatening summer flush faces, bulky chests, white Ts, dark Hollywood grins. One dry-out trip is like the next for the melancholic, life backbencher, AA junkie, left side of body still setting off metal detectors and nightmares of flying dragons across tanglescapes.

Could Mick, after all of this, really be delicate, ephemeral, *coming and going like dew*? Like fading photographs or the morning glints off dragon whorls, like fields of milkweed and dandelions beheaded by a slighting breeze, like the rustling ghosts of emptied summer fairgrounds, battlefields, like untethered balloons, Huey views, like blinking skies, morning tears, like Handsome Cousin and me and six under fire.

Miss Aubergine

Purple you go, a green dunce cap
atop your head. Your nerves so raw,
your envy-tinged core, all pudding flayed
as smooth, or soon, as Baba Ghanoush.

This place is green, is promising
full sun, sweet shade, the slow-
slow move of fellow seeds
on fellow vines — but not for you.

Miss Aubergine, in a rush to see,
be seen, to pull free first
mix and mingle, roast replete with
yesterday's garlic, tahini, and mint.

Neither Noir

Little sister
nutty as loon
drug-steeped and nude
with ex-cons and goons.
Would big sis be wrong
to lock her away
or drop kick her ass
for tagging along?

What if all slaps
to beautiful blondes
—slap sister, slap daughter,
slap mother, slap niece—
produced genealogy
inherently wrong
—slap tinker, slap doctor,
slap Indian chief?

And what if dear Laura
were shot after all?
Would Waldo and Copper
retire to soak
and together share many
a sweet bubble bath
with witty froth banter
twixt whiskeys and soap?

Crimetown and tough guys,
femme fatale swoons,
sweet silvery noir
shake this nonnoir of noon.

Nooners

I.

Time for a stretch
time for a burger and a papaya juice
time for a walk to clear the mind.

If I take Robert Lowell
we'll walk around the same
fourteen blocks and never eat.
He won't answer my questions
but disappear in the first cathedral/bar
to sequester his thoughts.

If I take James Schuyler
we will walk and wander
direction determined
by day's street flow.
He will likely question my answers
and we may disappear
like stars and years,
like blooms in drinking glasses
like fresh shores recently unwaved
our anxieties relicted by word play.

2.

Another noon of high-rise mad men
season summer/fall, with Frank O'Hara being
read at bar as a sign, perhaps, of—

meditations in an emergency
or just stray thoughts of James Deans
and the secrets cities of men again.

Lunch in dark bar, a reuben and pull,
in bullseye transom's split noonlight.
Jimmy is chasing down man-ray days.

In fog at end of bar, he reads aloud—
Auden in a funny voice—while I sit
young and green again and all atingle.

Past laundry

Past lanterns hung on strings, a wall of lanterns in as many hues as stars, as many shapes as towns along the Liffey. Past laundry hung on a long reed fence, a wall of color as varied, as breathless as the verdurous shades of Eire.

Past a blue table holding a thin tin pot, a pale reed hat, red noodle bowl and news print neither English nor Irish to a window sill and an incense stick burning in a Guinness bottle, smoke rising through peals of laughter.

Paul Muldoon et al.

I
Speak up, my dear—
the young woman's voice doesn't impale
doesn't make words turn in any way worth noting.
Not speaking well is criminal when stuck as we are
in harsh wooden seats, hot lecture hall
spring breeze a torment on
archful windows painted shut.
In truth, these pin-fall readings
are most needling when no words
stick to cushion the prick of splinters
dropped in whispers and chins.

II
Next the young buck does better read.
Speak up, friend, come dirty, come clean.
But while his word are decipherable
they do not, I fear, stand as his own—
except the jokes, the asides void of middle.
He reads his mentor passing well and collages—
stellar lines from women primed—
and he does from their heights rappel—
yet his own are mere giggles
scenarios comedic and slight
classical allusions as tittering glitz.

III
Paul Muldoon
takes the stage
looks up
speaks up
same hard wood
same windless room
yet his words break
smolder, threaten flame
until outcrawling come
rare pesty things.

Pietà

The child stays close, arranging kindling by sex. Strange days, shades of Ancien Régime and castle keep. C'est la vie, she squeaks, selecting the male twig from the female with much deliberation. Her art is great and when I tease, she chides, shaking her finger in morality play. I rest, bound by blankets near her and our hearth. Still, teasing is an easy joy. I mock her and she responds "silly old thing" and turns away.

Her tiny hedgehog sounds are cupping blows to deep congestion, dim secret cellars to which she—and she alone—holds bright, brassy keys.

Pining

The smell of pines—
and their needling resonance—
that's what the evening brings.

I want to love this lovely place
but make the mistake of asking for fireflies
which makes my cousins laugh:
"Silly! Not in California,
don't you know nothing in muddleland."
Even though I was born in Sacremento
and they were born in Springfield, Mo.

Once-cousins devising sandscapes—
brittle, fleet monuments toward which we,
as green and foreign as we are,
incline. Perhaps our bendability is
the pines we all spring from,
perhaps our green is meant
for cut and graft, to sway
in shifts of wind and view.

I will not see these cousins again, ever,
but they sit as tiny pine cones on my
window sill, neither seed nor fruit,
bark grails for long-lost, once-worlds.

Reptilian

1
I live to throw you off the scent
in games of love and games of chance.
It's in the throw my power lies
to lay in wait to best you and
to best you is no idol threat.

2
Lover man can barely wait to slip away
with serpent ease unless I prick him in his sleep
formaldehyde and pickling mix
to pith his brain or trap in glass
as paper weight for holding down
hosts on hosts of reptile men.

3
If not writ large can pleasure last
past the spasm, past the weight
the gravity as feet swing free
hit the floor in startled haste
cutting trapdoors, hatching chores.
A moment's ease is if and when
the door swings wide, love slithers in.

Schoolgirl

She somersaults through dawn, through
noon, and with dusk tosses mocking
banter off the warehouse
roof overlooking Newtown Creek.

Up with her artist boyfriend
on the parapet edge their
legs dangle and flutter—like hearts
or pigeons—at the precipice.

She imagines falling—
sees and fears her own
potential—and feels it a miracle
when there is no fall but only

a glimmer of orange-red-plum
and one white wisp of cloud
floating across sky
in the oily water below.

She thinks how happy, perfect
how it hurls her on not to fall,
to be left still laughing high above
like some rare, daring pioneer.

No fall but late at night she will
tumble into a deep, harrowed sleep
tangled up in her too big bed and
her too big-sky contentedness.

Sea Change

for Emlyn

Her thoughts are not mine now.
She stands apart
dancing in moonlight
head haloed in music
body vanguard to thought.

Her dreams are not mine now.
She dreams clandestinely
moving in her dreams—I imagine—
as she moves in mine
which I preserve, clandestine too
in tissue and cedar.

Life is more and more my own
now that she stands apart.
Dancing over head
dreaming through sun and moon
holding me a moment and then at bay
breaking waves in her sea change
much as my heart.

Sequoia

Devour, dent, wreck, atwist
waiting for an evening breeze
which might evoke brief breath-
lessness then oceans of release.

Fire, cracks, death—a bit—
enough to glean the holes within.
Heartwood, burls, threat—and yet—
enough to name the things to miss.

Sequoia anchor, biding time.
They sing their stance,
their standing green
in spite of match or lightening strike
in spite of all we'll ever know
old-growth wood runes know
ever more.

Songs

Saturday night, long awaited songs from Love Market. These songs are seeds and earth: girls hide and sing, boys search and sing, mothers and fathers wait, hum, remember. Only grand ones and surrounding hills know these songs in full bloom.

The hills rising above Sunday Market are terraced like grand faces—sun-softened, furrowed ground. Sunday Market songs are fragrant, windborne petals. These songs are shared through tea and smoke, through slow walks home, and the star-stitched promise of Love Market.

Standard Model:
The Physics of Weak Attraction

Lovers spin to
anti-love
a familiar
coupling constant.

Wane up to down
the you and me;
a stalwart switch
to you and she.

Strange meeting, mix
as the barkeep shouts
"Here's three pints
for three old friends!"

Our red and green
her charming blue
palettes of play be-
tween our watery set.

Summer Turbulence

Lightening/thunder popping up
from kernel clouds
from sea shore blankets
from summer stirred
rumblings, simply told
as
solstice zeal keeps
popping up
from cool, dark sands
from dry, grass dunes
from dark, cool theaters
from out of
nowhere, simply told
from summer heat
as
saturated air hits
saturated heat
40,000 feet or less
above the shimmery
halcyon shores.

Surrogates

Found
put back in play
with no blood spilt
but still ...
what better art
if blood had been
if not blood then
connection, fate
if not blood then
a covenant
to bind or break;
but this is specious
sanguinity
when loss is never
mine to own
but only let.

Territories

Our lost pine sways were seeking wisdom. The tallest named my mother's clan—in whispers green and bitter.

From the deep caverns of a mountain mouth, language seeped: mumbled sea stories, nascent poems, the soft breath of people.

Five nations shrank to palm size stars, dropping axes and jutting jaws, seeding the sky with their alphabet bones.

But afraid to weave a fish net, pecan bowl, woolen rug, to name a game, a dance, a song, a spirit from his past, my grandfather's reservations disclaimed even the gentlest casts of borrowed land.

Trace

The greens—kelly, lime, grass, sage—wrap round oak, privet, bay, the weeping holly and fig. Butter-blush glows—camellia, magnolia, wisteria—fall from bush, tree, trellis, gate. And the blues are sun-warm, perfectly round and expectant, navy yolks floating in heavy cream.

Light lands everywhere like engrams or letters or exams let fly in June. Light sifted through summer's heavy, gold-cast pools flourishes and fades, so slow, so delicately slow into paisley whirls when September stirs and threatens.

Ah, winding lanes: old fences, walls, cream field stones, bricks lichen blue, wrought iron palisades and spikes—fleur de lis favored but sometimes pilgrim pale and curlicue—and white washed wood, pickets knee-high for wood gnomes and fairies, criss-crossed between towers or potting sheds, undulating white wave froth and finish trim to lanes tattered as lace. Old green, old winding, old worries, young days.

And there a trace of a mock-tragic child. Tumbling from garden to lane by an aversion to sleep and that needing to know, yet what stays known longest and best is little but the lane and, perhaps, a bower with a patch of cool green on warm soil while everywhere lavender skies rustle waking and rewaking day on day.

Pause, resist, know what waits, behind eyelids, behind dreams for hours on end of bower palette and boundary lines. One moment's longing for creaking gates and breeze-chasing leaves, for lanes that wind just enough that one never knows where memory waits, which is the only passage back, the only ethos I'll likely claim.

Untriptych

Siren, wife, mistress, sometimes we think of her less, that is, we speak of her less as you and I bear solemn, silent the sort of exposures embattled comrades share. And friends when looking into our face, our time-worn, social face, imagine her shadowed there, but when we look we just see you and me (sans she) and our abandonment.

We share warmth, you and I, much as we once shared a kingdom in her arms only to find her secret weapon the courage to vacate, an unTrojan horse of hollow and quake. It is an embarrassing defeat, empathy worn as double yoke pulling the donkey cart of our mutual cuckoldry. We cherish the strain, the gravity of it, each other. You and I, comrade, say we can't imagine living without the effort of dragging yourselves around, can't imagine not imagining those past battles when all were fully armed. But more we can't imagine the brilliance of her escape.

But you, me, we need to try. Try to imagine how sweet, bitter, how complete her flight, imagine a deliverance from this endless exposure, where once a set of triple views hinged, unhinged.

Let us unfold, brother, unsuccumb. Let you and I for once be one, undone, man, be one without the other.

Watercress

Lucky ladies, a miracle how they stay plumb when the meadow is hobble-hoofed and wryly cast as steep-cut banks give way to Big River. Merry maidens path hand-span wide, next trick perhaps the head of pins. Their bovine grace leaves fallow fields a-fluttering. Vestal glade once heifer proof is live-wire gone since buckjump spree so sweet candied shoots beckon as star-brights wink from nebula green: yellow yarrow, red-pink buckwheat, blue-eyed weed.

The herd meanders its milky ways as pebble shoal gurgles wet siren tones: careful steps, sand soil shifts. Adventure. Bounty. Oceans of threat. One third of herd are river bound, one third demure from back creek sip, last third happy in cottonwood and willow shade. The Big River is mindful just of her lovely pour and flux, her talents at sculpting bluffs, meadows, woods at whim.

Brahman cows, pleasure bound, wade in water udder deep. River swift winkles and panic sets. Cows lunge benimbled knees kicking free. Content and cooled their ethos pays. River crew dally into troves of watercress, a rare rich find they share with midge and scud, darting brookies. Soon enough they will retake their wayward steps, join sisters in midday shade.

Hoof holes fill, loose cresses swim, and River is all mirth and marvel as she sculpts away.

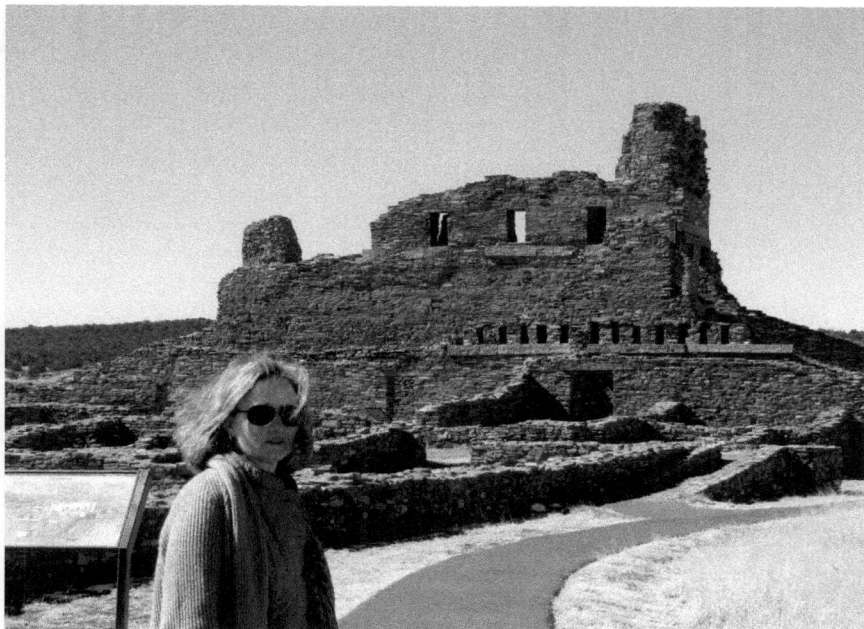

C. R. Resetarits was born in Sacramento, California, raised in St. Louis, Missouri, and has spent large chunks of time living in various cities along the Eastern seaboard and even a stint in England. Her migratory life and attempts at nesting are in part responsible for the poems in *Brood*. There is as well a brooding over the early loss of her mother and subsequent flight of her maternal grandfather—a man raised in the Oklahoma Indian Territories by his cowboy (read Cherokee) father and traditional (read Creek) mother—who never seemed comfortable with either his heritage or her (their) loss. C. R.'s poems, fiction, and essays have appeared in numerous journals and anthologies. This is her first collection of poetry. She currently lives in Faulkner-riddled Oxford, Mississippi.